Meadow Creek
BARBECUE EQUIPMENT
& ACCESSORIES ®

Meadow Creek Welding, LLC
New Holland, PA
Email: info@meadowcreekbbq.com
Website: MeadowCreekBBQ.com

We sell our products exclusively through our dealer network.
Use the dealer search on our website to find a sales rep who can give
you a quote, help you choose a smoker or grill, and take your order.

Contents

Customer Stories

I just completed my second cook on my TS120 and cannot believe what a great piece of equipment it is. For a family birthday I cooked four butts and eight beer can chickens. Everyone left full and happy.

Brad Mandell

Carterville, IL

"This is one of the best investments I have ever made. This would be a great business for someone. The best reward is when someone comes up and tells me, 'That is the best chicken I ever had; how do you keep it so good and moist?'"

Stewart Ellis

Clear Brook, VA

"I cook on a Meadow Creek PR60 Pig Roaster and a BBQ42 Chicken Cooker. Whether you're cooking chicken, pork butts, or even a whole hog, a Meadow Creek makes it easy and efficient."

Danny Lucas

Virginia

Welcome...

Thank you for your interest in the Meadow Creek Buyer Guide.

Our mission is to provide high quality smokers and grills that make amazing barbecue fun and easy—whether you are a backyard enthusiast, food service professional, fund-raiser, or competitor.

For well over 30 years, Meadow Creek Welding, LLC has been working hard to give customers a surprising level of durability, craftsmanship, and user-friendly design at an outstanding value for the price. Our equipment is hand-crafted in the Amish community of Lancaster County, PA by talented craftsmen who care about integrity and quality.

We've written this guide to help you define your presentation, cooking style, menu, and crowd size goals, and to choose a smoker or grill with confidence.

If you have trouble finding a dealer or getting the help you need, you can send me an email at info@meadowcreekbbq.com. You can also get a wealth of information about our products on our website at MeadowCreekBBQ.com.

We look forward to helping you turn your dreams into reality.

Sizzling regards,

Lavern Gingerich
Meadow Creek brand ambassador

A Culture of Excellence

So, why does Meadow Creek deserve your attention and respect? We could say a lot, but here are a few of the highlights:

- **Integrity:** Meadow Creek cookers are crafted within a culture of honesty, fairness, and diligent work ethics. Whether you're purchasing a Shoo-fly pie or a barbecue smoker, you will be treated right.

- **Awesomeness:** Our cookers are designed by barbecue experts and hand-made in the USA by talented welders and craftsmen. Every unit features outstanding workmanship to give you an amazing barbecue experience.

- **Rock Solid Construction:** These cookers are commercial grade and heavy duty for many years of dependable catering, competing, or backyard cookouts.

- **Revolution:** Meadow Creek offers designs and features, such as double-sided grill grates and stainless steel grates on all models, that are usually not found in other cookers on the market.

- **Stainless Steel Grates:** Every Meadow Creek barbecue cooker comes standard with non-rusting T304 stainless steel grates. This eliminates the hassle of scrubbing rust off the grates and the possibility of rust contamination on your meat.

- **Value:** Apples to apples, Meadow Creek equipment gives you outstanding value for the price.

"Working with Meadow Creek has been a great experience. I really like the way you take care of people. I was very pleased with the way the BBQ was crated for shipment."

—**Bill Jones**, Martinez, CA

A Healthy Brand

Meadow Creek builds as many as 1,500 units per year, and every year we are forced to increase production to keep up with orders. In light of the ongoing demand and steady growth, we have committed to increasing our equipment output without sacrificing quality.

Our shop team has recently implemented a system called "one flow production" to streamline reordering supplies and parts, which helps to keep things running smoothly and efficiently.

We have added a state of the art drive-through paint room with a dryer in it. Instead of waiting a couple of days for paint to cure enough to wrap for shipping, this dryer shortens the dry time to several hours. With our new work flow and paint room, we could potentially build a grill one morning and prep it for shipping by the end of the day.

Our new work flow and systems have increased production by 30% and given us empty spaces in the shop for future expansion. Between the increased production and the available workspace for new employees, we have the potential to double production with the same size shop.

Meadow Creek has become a healthy and stable brand, growing from the inside out. With all the changes we've implemented, we are better able to serve the market with shorter lead times and more focus on ongoing improvement.

Who Is Meadow Creek For?

Meadow Creek Is For People Who
Like to Play With Fire

Most of Meadow Creek's grills and smokers are charcoal and wood fired, so as a rule, Meadow Creek is for people who like to play with fire. Gas and electric are fine ways of cooking, but generally what you use when you need automation and push button performance—or don't have time or the desire to play with fire.

We often talk about the excellent performance of Meadow Creek's offset smokers and how well they hold a consistent temperature, but this is in reference to charcoal and wood burners in general. You'll still need to tend the fire, adding fuel to keep it on track as it burns down, and your fire will die out if neglected. After the cook, you'll have ashes to clean out of your firebox. But for those of us who love to play with fire—who find meaning and fulfillment in keeping watch over the firebox—it's just a part of what we do.

> I have to say that my TS250 is everything that I expected and more! It holds the temps like a dream and does not burn much wood at all. I have had 3 BBQ cooks with it cooking ribs, pork loin, and a turkey so far. Each cooked very well and had great flavor. I think the best part is being able to get it going and set the temperature and go do other jobs knowing the temps will hold. The quality in Meadow Creek cookers is top notch. —*Russell Welkley*

The magic of chicken grilling over a charcoal fire on a Meadow Creek Chicken Cooker is something you have to experience to appreciate—the smells, the sizzle, the heat, the grease, the smooth action of the rotating sandwich grates, and the perfect, delicious barbecue.

Meadow Creek Is For People Who
Love the Cooking Experience

If all you want is the "eating experience", meaning you "cook because you have to" in order to enjoy good barbecue, do yourself a favor and buy a pellet smoker with a digital thermostat or something else congruent with modern living. There's no shame in that. But if you find joy in mastering the perfect balance of draft and fuel, Meadow Creek is an awesome choice.

This past Saturday I cooked for our church group on my PR60. I cooked a case of beautiful pork butts that came out perfect on a 11 hour cook at 225 degrees. Being "old school" in my cooking techniques, I still use a burning barrel and use hickory and oak wood coals to fire the PR60. Where most people use charcoal and load their PR down with charcoal, I watch my temp and fire it up accordingly with hardwood coals. Besides making wonderful BBQ that people come back for seconds for, the old burning barrel is a perfect place for friends hang around and visit, which is the best part of a BBQ event.

The PR60 is a wonderful cooker and it can be used in many ways to cook good food on. It does a great job holding a constant temperature regardless of what you are using as fuel. —*Charlie Benton, Casar, NC*

Appreciate Integrity

Meadow Creek is founded on honesty and the Golden Rule: "Do to others what you wish they would do to you." If something breaks in shipping or the customer is disappointed in any way, Meadow Creek always goes the extra mile to take care of these situations.

> I really appreciate the versatility of the SQ36. The only problem I had was breaking the stub handle off one of the draft doors on the firebox. Lavern and Marlin were great about it! They had a new set of spiral handle doors made for me and shipped out no charge! The new doors are installed, they look great, and they will never break again! Thanks, guys!
>
> —Tom Stover, Kalamazoo, MI

Meadow Creek Is For People Who

Expect Excellence

Not quality as in a lame cliche, but the real thing. Meadow Creek cookers are handmade in New Holland, PA by talented craftsmen who are satisfied with nothing less than excellence. The heavy steel construction, smooth welds, handsome designs, and amazing performance are all part of the quality you can expect with Meadow Creek.

> I'm really impressed with the quality of this equipment, and so is everyone else who stops to look at it too. This past weekend I fired it up and cooked four pork butts, eight racks of St. Lewis style ribs, and a case of whole chicken legs. They turned out the best I've ever made, no exaggeration! These cookers make a seasoned professional out of an amateur. This was well worth the wait.
>
> —Jim from JD's Smoky Pit BBQ

> Probably the best thing about the Meadow Creek BBQ26S is its versatility. I can load it with charcoal and hickory chunks, close the lid, and adjust the dampers to extend the cook time out to an hour and a half for some nicely smoked BBQ Chicken. I also have the fixed charcoal grate and griddle. By setting the charcoal pan at the higher location the cooker makes a superb charcoal grill. It cooks some of best steaks I've done in the last 40 years. Same goes for the griddle. —*John Moyers*

"The smoker keeps a constant temperature like a dream."
Blake, Terre It Up Catering

> The smoker keeps a constant temperature like a dream and the roaster even doubly so. The last time I cooked a whole pig on a borrowed rotisserie, Mother Nature got ugly and it was a flaming nightmare. This time she was fully willing to put the Meadow Creek PR60G to the test. I set the temp, loaded the pig and down came the rain and a fair bit of wind. So I adjusted the gas to keep the heat flowing and from then on it was sweet dreams with me only getting up twice through the night to see that everything was running smoothly. Thank you, Meadow Creek, for building such solid equipment and thanks to Yoder's staff for the excellent service.
>
> —*Blake Anderson, Chef/Owner, Terre It Up Catering, Alberta, Canada*

Here is a summary of the four categories of Meadow Creek cookers, so you have a point of reference when we mention them later.

PIG ROASTERS

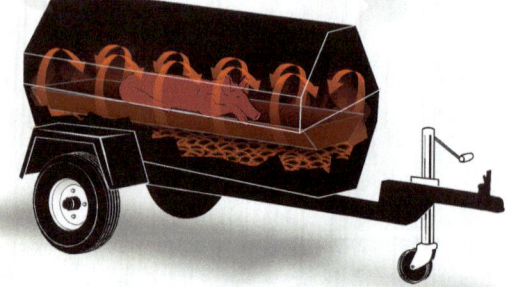

Besides whole pigs, you can cook a huge variety of foods on a Meadow Creek pig roaster—easily and efficiently. The drip pan creates indirect heat, and the roaster's design makes it easy to hold a consistent temperature. On charcoal units, you can add enough charcoal to last for 12-14 hours and with the help of a Guru temperature controller, you can safely leave it unattended while you catch a night's sleep.

You can use a pig roaster to cook anything you would do in a regular smoker. These pig roasters are a perfect solution if you want to cook whole pigs and don't want to purchase a second cooker for general smoking.

The optional grill pan turns this roaster into a direct-heat grill for easily grilling hundreds of burgers and steaks in a short time.

Usage Summary: This pig roaster is a great choice if you want to cook large whole pigs, plus smoke any other cuts low and slow. You can even grill foods over direct heat if you add an optional grill pan.

Fuel Types: Available in gas or charcoal/wood fired.

Sizes: We have highway trailer models and those made to move by hand. Sizes range from 36" to 72". Great for backyarders and big-time caterers.

SMOKERS

Meadow Creek offers several types of smokers, including their classy reverse flow tank smokers. All their smokers are charcoal/wood fired and make cooking with fire fun and easy.

A common problem with cheap offset smokers is inconsistent temperature—it can be a real battle maintaining the fire for long cooks. Our high-end charcoal and wood-fired smokers make it a breeze to crank out amazing barbecue while still giving you the fun of poking coals.

Meadow Creek's tank smokers have reverse flow draft (see the illustration below) and rounded tank ends for the best performance and class in offset stick burners. Meadow Creek's box smoker is extremely efficient, compact, and dependable and built so well it can smoke dry for making jerky.

Usage Summary: If you want to cook with indirect heat, but occasionally cold smoke cheese and cook over direct heat (with the optional grill pan), one of these is a good choice.

Fuel Types: Available in charcoal/wood fired models.

Sizes: The BX50T, TS120, TS250, and TS500 models each come built on a highway trailer. The other smokers are made to move around by hand, but you can order any model mounted on a custom trailer. Sizes range from smaller backyard models to the 500-gallon TS500.

CHICKEN COOKERS

Known as the "chicken flippers", these Meadow Creek grills with rotating sandwich grates take barbecue fund-raising and backyard grilling to a whole new level. Double-sided rotating grates make it easy to turn the entire rack of meat with one hand. The stainless steel grates are non-rusting and easy to maintain for long years of use.

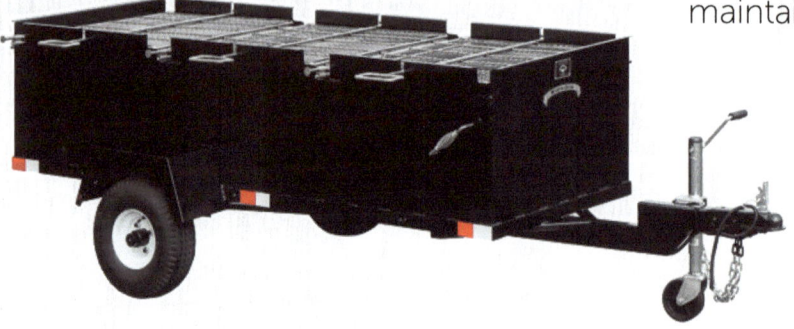

There are two common problems when cooking bone-in chicken: Over direct heat, your chicken will tend to dry out before it's done; on an offset smoker, unless you are really good, the skin will be rubbery. The distance between the fire and the grate in these Meadow Creek grills eliminates this problem, and there is no better way to grill chicken for crowds!

These grills make it easy to grill large amounts of perfectly done chicken, potatoes, and sausage links even on your first try. You can also grill things like burgers and steaks that require a more intense fire if you raise the charcoal pan (brackets are custom on the larger units).

Usage Summary: A chicken cooker is a good choice if you want to easily grill lots of amazing chicken, but you also want the option to grill other foods.

Fuel Types: Available in charcoal/wood fired models.

Sizes: Sizes range from the small 26" BBQ26 for backyard use to a custom order trailer with as many pits as you want.

GRILLS

If you want to do a lot of direct heat grilling, such as burgers, steaks, and sausages, in your restaurant, catering business, or fund-raising projects, these commercial grills are a great choice for years of constant use.

They come in two sizes, and you can choose between gas or charcoal. All the models have height adjustable, stainless steel grates.

Usage Summary: If you need a grill that will handle hundreds of burgers and steaks on a daily basis, one of these grills will do an outstanding job for you.

Fuel Types: Available in gas or charcoal/wood fired models.

Sizes: 36" and 60"

Defining Your Goal

You may have plans to become anything from a serious backyarder to a professional caterer serving hundreds in a day. Once you define the four building blocks of your goal below, choosing your equipment will become a lot easier.

#1 – Presentation

Do you want to cook whole hogs for photo ops? Do you want the wow factor of showing up with a classic stick burner offset pit? Will you be making smoke on-site? Or is the presentation irrelevant?

#2 – Cooking Style

Learn the differences between direct heat, indirect heat, and semi-direct heat, and the common cooking styles within each category.

#3 – Menu

What do you dream of cooking? Mostly grilled chicken and sausage? Burgers and hotdogs? Smoked brisket and ribs? Or some of everything?

#4 – Crowd Size

Are you only cooking for a few people in your backyard, or are we talking big hungry crowds? The saying "tools of the trade" is never more true than when it comes to choosing the right size of equipment for the crowd you're tackling.

In the following pages, we'll cover each of these points to help you define your goal.

The Value of Presentation

Cooking outdoors is a rich tradition of community and social interaction. Everyone is drawn to the pitmaster, the pit, and the sizzling meat. In this age of automation, Meadow Creek excels at maintaining these core values of barbecue while giving us equipment that is fun and easy to use and capable of handling big crowds.

If presentation is not important to your goal, you can cook great barbecue in computer-controlled boxes, but if you dream of "working the pit" that is the center of attention at the party, Meadow Creek can help you reach that goal.

"People are impressed when they see what I'm cooking."

Wade Janes, Wild Wades BBQ & Grill, CA

"I do hog roasts and a five-foot grill on wheels is perfect."

Anthony Ginter, Campbellsville, KY

"We're proud of our Meadow Creek Smoker; it looks great behind our van."

Chris Polfus, Brady's Brewhouse, WI

The smoke and smell of grilling chicken on an open pit is intoxicating to the crowds.

Cooking Style

It's easy to get confused when terms like *barbecue*, *grilling*, and *smoking* are thrown around loosely and the lines between different cooking styles are blurred, but in this section, we're going to break it all down and help you define your cooking style.

There are many different styles of grills and smokers on the market, but they are all based on one of these three configurations:

1. Direct heat
2. Indirect heat
3. Semi-direct heat

Your presentation goal, as well as your menu and crowd size (covered later in this guide), will help determine your cooking style, but it is important to understand how cooking style affects the cooking experience as well as the finished product.

Example 1: You may have your heart set on a whole hog rotiserrie cooking style, but a Meadow Creek Pig Roaster cooks the same hog to perfection with a lot less hassle. You may still choose a rotiserrie for presentation's sake, but that's a personal choice you'll have to make.

Example 2: You can cook a chicken on an offset smoker, but the finished result is different than if you cook it over semi-direct heat. It's not that one is right and the other wrong, but understanding the nuances of each helps a lot when choosing your equipment.

The chart on the next page explains the differences between the three cooking configurations and some cooking styles within each category. In the following pages, we will explore these methods in more detail.

What About Cold Smoking?

When we talk about smoking meat, we are referring to hot smoking, the process of fully cooking raw meat and using smoke to flavor the meat. We recommend leaving cold smoking meat to the professionals, but cheese is a great item for cold smoking in the backyard. See "Cold Smoking Cheese."

INDIRECT	SEMI-DIRECT	DIRECT
The fire is offset in a separate box or separated from the meat with a baffle.	The fire is separated from the meat by horizontal or vertical distance.	No barrier between the fire and the meat. Most intense heat against the meat.

COOKING STYLES

- Offset "stick burners"
- Kamado grills with a heat deflector
- Charcoal-fired "bullet" smokers
- Charcoal-fired cabinet smokers
- Gas-fired smokers with wood chip smoke generator
- Electric smokers with sawdust disc smoke generator
- Pellet grills

- 2-zone cooking on any grill with a lid
- Deep pits with food grates at the top
- Upright barrels
- Rotisseries
- Gas grills with infrared grates

- The classic open park grills
- Charcoal-fired kettle grills with lid
- Gas grills
- Charcoal-fired ceramic grills

MEADOW CREEK EXAMPLES

Meadow Creek Pig Roasters, BX Smokers, and Tank Smokers	**Meadow Creek Chicken Cookers**	**Meadow Creek Grills** (BBQ36 and BBQ60) **and Chicken Cookers** (with charcoal pan raised)

This chart doesn't cover every cooking style in use today, but is designed to give beginners an overview of how common cooking styles relate to each other.

Indirect Cooking

You've probably heard of *low and slow* barbecue, *southern-style* barbecue, or "real" barbecue. People mostly use these terms to refer to indirect cooking, a method famous people use to cook award-winning brisket and ribs and win prestigious awards. The trophies and the size of their smokers can be intimidating at first, but indirect cooking is far from rocket science.

Low and slow is a popular indirect cooking style where meat is cooked at 225–250 degrees F for anywhere from a couple of hours to all day, depending on the cut. Cooking at higher temperatures is fairly common, too. In fact, indirect pellet grills can go from "low and slow" to high heat with the push of a button.

These meats are commonly cooked with indirect heat:

- Ribs
- Beef brisket
- Pork butts
- Whole chickens and turkeys
- Sausage
- Pork belly
- Whole pigs

Done right, low and slow barbecue is tender, juicy, and outrageous, and there are many exciting opportunities to creating amazing barbecue, such as catering events, backyard cookouts, family get-togethers, church and community functions, and fundraisers!

For fuel, many enthusiasts favor charcoal and wood, but there are plenty of propane or electric smokers on the market, especially small backyard models. These smokers try to capture the flavor produced on a classic stick burner by burning pellets, sawdust discs, wood chips, or wood splits in a smoke generator.

Indirect cooking should not be confused with cold smoking in a smoke house. People refer to indirect cooking as smoking, but smoke is only one element of amazing barbecue cooked on a smoker. Indirect cooking means fully cooking and storing the meat just as you would if you had cooked it in the kitchen. Of course, our work is greatly enhanced by cooking with wood or some kind of wood supplement; the flavor of a pork butt cooked for twelve hours over hardwood charcoal is incredible.

- **Offset smokers:** These cookers have a cooking area (oven) with a firebox on the side. The heat travels from the firebox into the oven and out the stack.

- **Reverse flow offset smokers:** These smokers hold a more consistent temperature than regular offset smokers. The heat travels from the firebox under a solid plate, enters the oven on the opposite end, drafts back toward the firebox end, and then exits through the stack.

- **Upright smokers:** There are many variations of this cooking style, but basi- cally the heat source is in the bottom of the smoker; heat travels from the bottom up, around a drip pan or heat deflector, past the meat, and out the vent(s).

Quality: The big box stores have not only brought us cheap shoes and groceries. Here in the US, you will find a variety of affordable, entry-level smokers at local hardware and department stores.

Some cheap smokers are a great investment, but do your research carefully. Would you rather spend $200 on an offset smoker that will rust out in several years and is hard to maintain during a long cook or invest $1,000+ in one that you can pass on to the next generation and is fun to use? There is a reason for the difference in price. If you're only researching online, compare the listed weights of the smokers, for example, and you will find that a higher-priced smoker generally has a lot more steel.

> **"Don't be tempted by those cookers that look like good offsets that you see in front of those big box stores. If you're paying under $500 for an offset, you're throwing money away."** —Greg MrVich, Ballistic BBQ

Capacity: Your crowd size may partly determine your cooking style. Many backyard smokers are quite small, but not too small if you can get by with four or five square feet of cooking space. (See the "Crowd Size" chapter.)

Automation: The main advantage of gas or electric smokers is automation. These will appeal to you if you just want to get the job done with the least work.

A pellet smoker is electric-powered, and temperature control is completely automated—all you have to do is set the thermostat and keep pellets in the bin. You can switch from low and slow to high-heat grilling with the push of a button. While you can't control the amount of smoke that is generated, more smoke is generated at low and slow temperatures. Even then, some users install an additional smoke generator to increase the density of the smoke, and Yoder Smokers has developed a pellet smoker with a bigger burner to duplicate the smoke density of an offset smoker. Pellet smokers are a great option for those who don't like to play with fire.

Another example is the Bradley electric smoker, which is also controlled by a thermostat and generates a set amount of smoke by burning sawdust discs. It's not very capable of cooking at high temperatures, so once it's loaded with meat, you'll be doing well if you can get the temperature in the oven up to 225. Overall it does a fine job of smoking, and it's automated.

If you want to cook with charcoal and wood, but also want some automation, consider adding an electronic temperature controller, such as the BBQ Guru. You can even get one that lets you monitor and control the temperature of your pit from your phone. The controller adjusts air flow as needed to maintain a constant temperature. If you add one of these to a well-built offset or cabinet smoker, you will reduce your fire maintenance even more.

Budget: Your equipment budget will vary greatly if you're looking to cook for profit versus cooking for a few people on the back deck. There are some fine inexpensive smokers out there, such as Weber's "bullet" smoker and Bradley's electric smoker that you can pick up for several hundred dollars. That may be a good starting point for you, but if you're really serious, why not dream big and step it up a notch?

Mobility: Where will you be cooking—at home or away? Ceramic cookers such as the Big Green Egg or Kamado Joe are easy to use, extremely versatile, and efficient, but they are heavy and rather fragile for travel. (See the chapter on "Mobility.")

Cooking style is a personal choice you'll have to make, and quality, capacity, automation, budget, and mobility are all factors to consider in addition to your *presentation* and *menu* goals.

"The greatest experience I've ever had with my Meadow Creek was cooking for Operation BBQ Relief out in New Jersey after Hurricane Sandy. My barrel ran around the clock for almost 40 hours, putting out over 2,000 pounds of chicken quarters and shoulders. The last day we were on-site is when the northeaster hit. Wind, heavy snow, and ice, and the old girl just kept on going. Knowing we were helping out some folks that really needed it made the whole trip worthwhile, and we could never have done it without our Meadow Creek TS250."

Pitmaster Johnny Van

Indirect Cooking Solutions

A well-built charcoal/wood-fired smoker is like a powerful 4x4 pickup truck—there is no shortage of heat or smoke. Besides, playing with fire will get you the badge of pitmaster a lot quicker than pushing buttons will! Meadow Creek's charcoal smokers feature great-looking designs, heavy-duty construction, non-rusting grates, smooth welds, secure latches, and most of all, a fun and easy cooking experience that will keep you fired for years to come.

Offset Smokers. Meadow Creek's reverse-flow offset smokers do an excellent job of holding the temperature for long cooks, and they look pretty cool too. The temperature will naturally rise and fall when you refuel or let it die down, but properly fired, they are like a ship in water traveling full steam ahead; it takes a strong current to throw the temperature off track.

> Cooking with my Meadow Creek cookers is the best fun I've had in many years. I can honestly say they're the best investments I've ever made. I've seen people using other smokers, and they seem to spend a lot of time adjusting this or that. With a Meadow Creek cooker, I get it set, then just sit back and let it do its thing. They have to be some of the best-made cookers out there. One day I hope to buy a big custom trailer unit.
>
> I also like that help for the Meadow Creek cookers is just a phone call away.
>
> Phil Janssens, North Wales, PA

Box Smokers. Box smokers have been doing well at competitions, and backyarders love them because they're compact, easy to use, and efficient to run. What really sets Meadow Creek's BX50 box smoker apart is the ability to use it with or without water! Unlike some cabinet smokers on the market, the BX50 works fine without water, which means you can use it for jerky. The water does help stabilize the temperature, but it does a very good job without water too.

> I highly recommend the Meadow Creek smoker. It took some getting used to for me, but I love everything about it... Because I like to cook at night while I sleep, I added a Guru and a 30 CFM fan; this works beautifully. I have been reading StoryQue magazine and trying lots of new things. This BX50 Box Smoker has opened up a whole new dimension for me. The water jug works great. I've smoked some jerky dry, and my next adventure is a cured bacon. I mostly cook butts, brisket, and ribs, but I am learning with each new cooking.
>
> Brian, Gaffney, SC

Pig Roasters. Meadow Creek's pig roasters are known for their simple design and ease of use. The advantage in a pig roaster is that you can cook a whole pig on it, plus use it for cooking nearly any kind of meat you would put in an offset smoker.

A gas pig roaster is a great choice if you want automation and less clean-up. To cook with smoke on the gas models, you can add the optional chip tray or charcoal pan. However, even the charcoal models will run all night on auto-pilot with the help of an electronic temperature controller. (See the Pig Roaster options in "Making Sense of the Options" for more details.)

In some cases an offset smoker may work better than a pig roaster for cooking low and slow, but if you want to cook whole hogs and don't want more than one cooker, this is definitely a great choice. It basically comes down to your cooking style preference and whether you want more room for whole hogs.

> I own two restaurants and have been in this business for over 25 years. Having pig roasts is probably the most popular thing we've done, and the Meadow Creek Pig Roaster is an incredible piece of equipment. **We were very surprised to see the quality of the product, as well as how easy it is to operate.** Our customers love being part of the process and seeing the pig (and other items) cooking. The smell alone drives people crazy. I just wanted to say thank you for your help and for providing me with such a quality piece of equipment. **It has made us more profitable and more unique.**
>
> **John McCarthy**
> **Casey's Publichouse, Holliston, MA**

Semi-Direct Cooking

Semi-direct heat is similar to indirect, but instead of using a physical barrier to diffuse the heat, the food is spaced at a greater vertical or horizontal distance from the fire than with direct heat.

- **Vertical distance:** Some cookers, such as the popular Pit Barrel Cooker and Meadow Creek's Chicken Cookers, use a semi-direct configuration with extended vertical distance above the fire.

- **Horizontal distance (two-zone):** On any grill with a lid, build a fire on one side of the grill (on a gas grill, use only one of the burners) and put your meat on the opposite side. The disadvantage of this method is that you can't use the entire grate, so this only works when you don't need much capacity. Furthermore, some cuts are easier to master with true indirect heat.

Boston butts over semi-direct heat on a Weber Kettle Grill

Semi-direct can be used as a low and slow cooking style for cuts that are normally done with indirect heat. A two-zone fire is also helpful when cooking some thicker items over direct heat.

Semi-direct heat is the best way to cook bone-in chicken or turkey. Over direct heat, it tends to dry out before it's done; on an offset smoker, unless you are really good, the skin will be rubbery. The semi-direct setup in a Meadow Creek chicken cooker eliminates this problem and makes it easy to grill perfect chicken with crispy skin every time. (More on this in "Direct Heat Cooking".)

Other Semi-Direct Cooking Styles

A rotisserie is also somewhat semi-direct since the surface of the meat is constantly moving away from the hottest point of the fire. Infrared grates on gas grills also fit into the semi-direct category and are a big help in cooking thicker cuts uniformly on a regular grill.

Direct Cooking

In direct-heat cooking there is no barrier between the fire and the meat, so the heat is much more intense than with indirect cooking. We call this method grilling. The high heat of the fire cooks your food quickly, browning the surface and tempting everyone in the neighborhood.

These foods are excellent grilled:

- Burgers
- Steaks
- Hot dogs
- Brats
- Pork chops
- Party wings
- Chicken thighs, legs, breasts
- Sliced potatoes and squash

You could cook all of the above with indirect heat, but they are better cooked quickly over *direct* or *semi-direct* heat. If you can save time, retain more of the juice, and have grill marks and crispy skin to boot, why not?

Grilling Challenges

A common challenge when cooking with direct heat is the risk of overcooking the surface of the meat before the center is fully cooked. For example, if you try to grill bone-in chicken thighs and legs with direct heat only, it will be impossible to cook it properly unless you have a way to reduce the heat for part of the cook.

Another challenge with grills is that they need to endure a lot of heat, and many cheap grills rust through quickly.

Grilling Solutions

Chicken Cookers: A Meadow Creek Chicken Cooker with rotating grates makes it easy to grill perfect chicken and lots of it, if you choose a trailer model. The secret with these is the semi-direct configuration—its vertical distance between the fire and the grate. And they are made of heavy steel that will survive many years of heavy use.

You can convert the BBQ42 and BBQ26S (backyard models) to direct heat by raising the charcoal pan. The grate won't be able to rotate while the pan is in this raised position, but you can hook the grate on the lid in an open position and cook anything

Chicken legs over
semi-direct heat on
a Meadow Creek
Chicken Cooker

that works best with direct heat, such as burgers and steaks.

You can even add an optional griddle for frying eggs, pancakes, bacon, burgers, fries, and frog legs.

Note: If you want to raise the pan on the trailer model chicken cookers, you'll have to ask for the optional *pan brackets* and single-sided *flat grates*.

Shrimp kabobs over direct heat on a
Meadow Creek Chicken Cooker

These chicken cookers are extremely versatile. The smaller units are a lot of fun to have on the back porch and the trailer units make it easy to cook for hundreds.

Grills: Meadow Creek's BBQ36 and BBQ60 are made for heavy daily use. If you want to do a lot of direct heat grilling, such as burgers, steaks, and hotdogs in your restaurant, catering business, or fund-raising projects, these grills will give you years of dependable use.

Pig Roasters: Meadow Creek's pig roasters are extremely versatile and built to last. You can add a grill pan to any of the pig roasters to convert it to direct heat. For example, a PR60 gives you grilling surface 2' wide and 5' long.

Offset Smokers: You can cook with direct heat on Meadow Creek's offset smokers by adding an optional grill pan. On the tank smokers, you remove the bottom grate and slide in the grill pan. So if you want an offset that lets you smoke in style but easily converts to a direct heat grill, one of these would be a great choice.

I received the trailer and have been working very hard to get everything up and running for my BBQ business, I'm really impressed with the quality of this equipment, and so is everyone else who stops to look at it too. This past weekend I fired it up and cooked four pork butts, eight racks of St. Louiss style ribs, and a case of whole chicken legs. They turned out the best I've ever made, no exaggeration!!! These cookers make a seasoned professional out of an amateur. This was well worth the wait.

Thanks again,

Jim
JD's Smoky Pit BBQ

Cold Smoking Cheese

Cheese is a popular item to smoke cold. Cold smoking uses a steady flow of smoke and no heat. You can control the flavor and intensity of the smoke flavor with the following:

- Type of wood (chips, pellets, etc)
- Length of time in smoke
- Density of the smoke

One challenge when smoking cheese is keeping the smoker cool enough in spite of warm outdoor temperatures and the heat from the fire you use to generate smoke.

The best way to cold smoke is with a smoker that generates smoke without heat, such as the Bradley Electric smoker, or by adding a smoke generator, such as the pellet-fired A-MAZE-N or a homemade "fire can," to your offset smoker or any covered grill.

Meadow Creek's smokers are a great solution if you want to smoke a lot of meat and occasionally smoke cheese during the cooler part of the year.

Menu

Hopefully, by now some ideas are forming around your presentation and cooking style goals. We've already discussed specific meats in the previous chapters, but it's time to get really specific about what you plan to cook with your new equipment.

It's likely you want to cook a variety of cuts, and that's great. Sometimes this can be done with one versatile cooker; other times, it may take more than one cooker, such as a Meadow Creek tank smoker with a chicken cooker mounted to the front for both indirect and direct cooking.

The chart on the following page illustrates which category of Meadow Creek equipment you will need for each food item listed, and the recommended cooking style for each one.

If you are having trouble understanding which Meadow Creek equipment will help you reach your goals, feel free to ask. We will be happy to walk you through it.

Meat Recommendations Chart

Meats	Pig Roasters	BBQ Smokers	Chicken Cookers	Flat Top Grills
Whole Pigs	Indirect	Indirect		
Large Cuts of Meat, such as a quarter beef	Indirect	Indirect		
Pork Butts	Indirect	Indirect		
Beef Briskets	Indirect	Indirect		
Beef or Pork Ribs	Indirect	Indirect	Semi-Direct	Direct
Pork Loin and Tenderloin	Indirect	Indirect		
Whole Chickens and Turkeys	Indirect	Indirect	Semi-Direct*	
Bone-in Chicken Pieces	Indirect	Indirect	Semi-Direct	
Skinless, boneless chicken breasts and thighs	Direct**	Direct**	Semi-Direct	Direct
Burgers, hotdogs, steaks, chops, and sausage links	Direct**	Direct**	Semi-Direct	Direct
Vegetables	Indirect	Indirect	Semi-Direct	Direct

Color Code:

Awesome	Works Fine	Not Recommended

*Butterflied **With Grill Pan

Crowd Size

Timing and capacity are two potential stress factors in cooking for crowds, so defining your crowd size is an important part of the research.

A lot of backyard grills and smokers can handle a couple dozen people at a time—no sweat; but if you're aiming to feed 100 or 250 people at a time, there's nothing like having the right tools for the job.

This chart shows roughly how many people you can feed with each model of Meadow Creek cooker *per batch*. On the direct heat models, you can easily do multiple batches to multiply the capacity.

Some of these numbers are based on pulled pork which is very space efficient. Items like ribs and chicken won't feed as many people per area of cooking space.

Refer to the charts on the following pages for meat capacities of each model.

Model	Number of People
PIG ROASTERS	
PR42	75–100
PR60	175–250
PR72	300–400
SMOKERS	
PR36	50–75
SQ36	50–75
BX25*	75
BX50*	200
TS70*	100–175
TS120*	250
TS250*	400
TS500*	900–1000
CHICKEN COOKERS	
BBQ26	10–15
BBQ42	30–50
BBQ96	100** or 150–175***
BBQ144	200** or 325–400***
GRILLS	
BBQ36****	35
BBQ60****	60

*Cooking pork butts.
**Cooking chicken halves.
***Cooking chicken legs.
****Cooking burgers.

Capacity Charts

Pig Roasters

These charts show the differences between Meadow Creek's pig roaster models. The main differences in the different models are fuel type, size, and trailer versus pull-around. Choose from charcoal/wood or gas fired and three sizes: 42", 60", and 72". The larger units are available on a trailer.

Model	Fuel Type		Pig Size			Type	
	Charcoal	Gas	100 lb.	200 lb.	275 lb.	Pull-around*	Trailer
PR42	●		●			●	
PR60	●			●		●	
PR72	●				●	●	
PR42G		●	●			●	
PR60G		●		●		●	
PR72G		●			●	●	
PR60T	●			●			●
PR72T	●				●		●
PR60GT		●		●			●
PR72GT		●			●		●

To move around by hand. Not mounted on a trailer for highway use.

Pig Roaster Meat Capacities

The 2nd Tier grate is optional and almost doubles the cooking surface.

Meats	PR42		PR60		PR72	
	Single	2nd Tier	Single	2nd Tier	Single	2nd Tier
Whole Pigs	100 lb	na	200 lb	na	275 lb	na
Racks of Ribs**	5–6	10–12	8–12	15–25	12–15	24–30
Whole Chickens	12–14	22–24	21–24	40–45	25–30	50–60
Hamburgers	40–45	70–80	70–75	135–140	85–90	160–175
Pork Butts	10–11	18–20	18–20	30–35	21–24	40–44

***Spare ribs lying flat. With the optional rib rack, you can cook ribs on edge.*

Smoker Capacities

Tank Smoker Meat Capacities

Meats	TS70	TS120	TS250	TS500
Pork Butts	7–8	21–22	31–32	64–65
Racks of Baby Back Ribs	7–8	15–18	26–34	50–60
Racks of Spare Ribs	6	12–14	18–22	35–40
Whole Briskets	5–6	13–14	19–22	46–50
Whole Chickens	12	30–31	45–47	100–105
Whole Pigs	20–25 lb.*	100 lb.*	200 lb.*	4 x 40 lb.*

SQ36 and PR36 Smoker Meat Capacities

Meats	Single Grate	2nd Tier Grate
Pork Butts	5–6	10
Racks of Spare Ribs	2–3	4–5
Whole Briskets	2	4
Chicken Halves	10–12	15–20
Whole Pigs	30–40 lb.*	na

*Dressed weight.

Box Smoker Meat Capacities

The BX25 comes standard with 3 grates and the BX50 with 4. See "Box Smoker Options" on page 49 to learn how the extra grates affect capacity.

Meats	BX25	BX50
Pork Butts	6	16
Racks of Baby Back Ribs	6	16
Racks of Spare Ribs	3	8
Racks of St. Louis Ribs	6	12
Whole Briskets	3	8
Brisket Flats	3–6	12–16
Chicken Halves	12	32

Grill Capacities

Meats	BBQ36	BBQ60
Burgers	40	70
Racks of Spare Ribs	3–4	5–6

Chicken Cooker Capacities

Meats	BBQ26	BBQ42	BBQ96	BBQ144
Chicken	15 lbs.	40 lbs.	120 lbs.	240 lbs.
Burgers	24	32	150	350
Racks of Spare Ribs	2	4–5	15–18	32–40

Gas or Charcoal?

We've already covered the pros and cons of various fuel types in "Cooking Styles" and "Who Is Meadow Creek For?" Here is a list of which Meadow Creek smokers and grills are gas and which are charcoal.

Gas Models

Meadow Creek cookers with a "G" in the model name are gas models.

- Pig roasters: PR42G, PR60G, PR60GT, PR72G, PR72GT. (You can add a wood chip tray to a gas pig roaster to give your meat some smoke flavor. Otherwise, it will be a lot like cooking meat in a regular oven.)
- Grills: BBQ36G and BBQ60G.

Advantages of Cooking With Gas

- Quick and easy—turn it on and it's on.
- No ash clean-up.
- Easy to control and maintain—handy for a long burn if you want to get some sleep or don't want to tend the fire.

Charcoal Models

Most of the models are charcoal-fired. You can supplement the fire with wood splits, chunks, or chips.

- Pig Roasters: PR36, PR42, PR60, PR60T, PR72, PR72T
- Smokers (all of them)
- Chicken Cookers (all of them)
- Grills: BBQ36 and BBQ60

Advantages of Cooking With Charcoal

- Amazing smoke flavor—even without wood, a good quality 100% hardwood charcoal will give your food that classic barbecue flavor.
- Fun—it takes some manual fire management to cook with charcoal, but who doesn't like to play with fire?

Mobility

Meadow Creek's trailer models are built on a road-worthy trailer with flush-mount LED lights for safe travel anywhere you need to go. A heavy duty jack makes it easy to level the trailer once it's in position. Each trailer comes with a VIN number and a certificate of origin is available upon request.

Some of the models are available either with or without a trailer frame. For example, the TS120P Smoker is similar to the TS120 Trailer Smoker, but it's on casters for those that simply need a patio model. We can also give you a custom quote for any of the units on a trailer or as a push-around model.

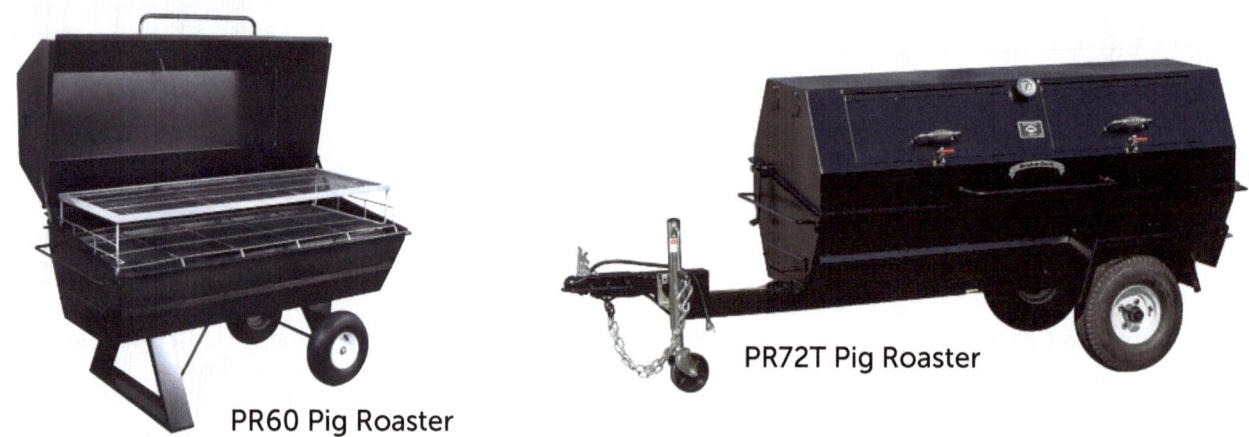

PR60 Pig Roaster

PR72T Pig Roaster

Of course, you can haul the smaller units on a trailer or the back of your truck if you strap them down well. But if you're on the road a lot, why not invest in a cool trailer model—or even a trailer with a custom arrangement of smokers and grills to suit your needs?

TS120 Smoker With BBQ26 Chicken Cooker

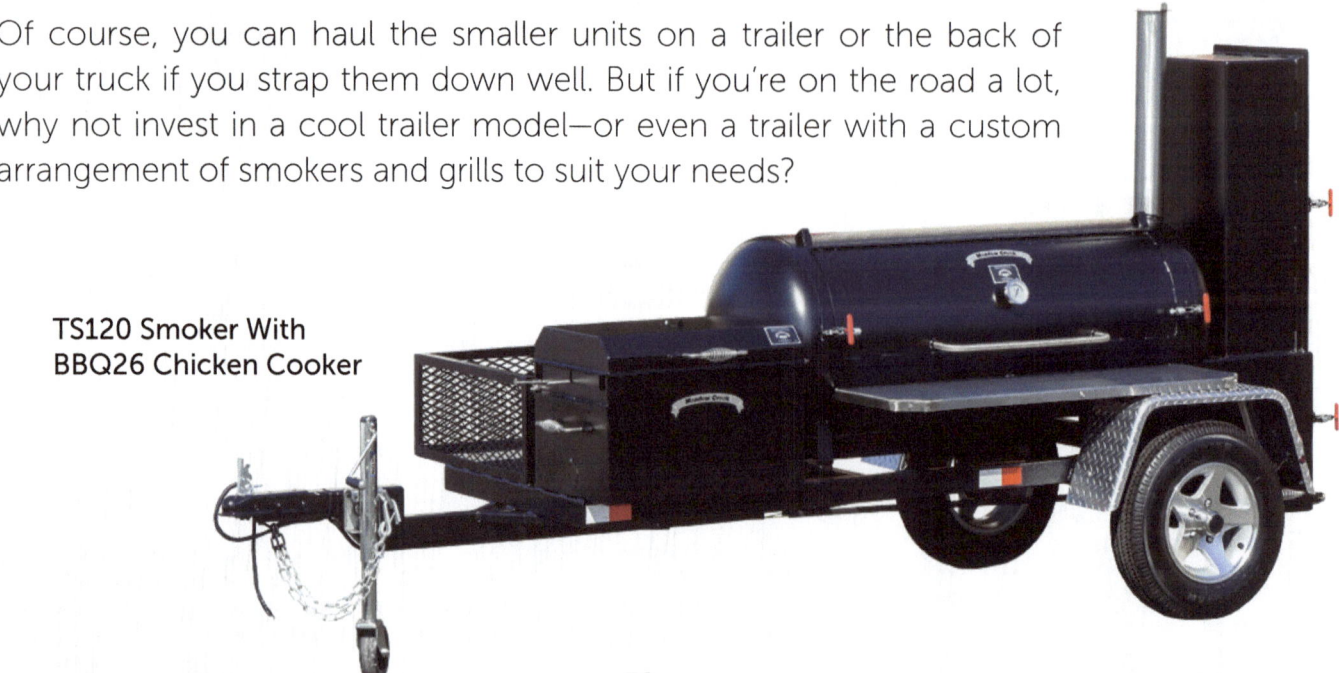

Making Sense of the Options

Meadow Creek offers an impressive list of options (upgrades) for expanding the usefulness of their smokers and grills. Hopefully the following explanations will help you decide which ones are a good investment for you.

- **Vinyl Cover.** These covers are Amish-made in Lancaster County from tough vinyl material. If you will be storing your cooker outside or even in a covered area, a vinyl cover will help to keep it clean and dry. Otherwise, it will rust sooner and take more maintenance.

Chicken Cooker Options

- **Flat Grate**. A flat grate is a single-panel grate that replaces the rotating sandwich grate. The "sandwich" grate that comes with every chicken cooker has a set distance between the two panels, and some foods are either too thin or too thick to put in the sandwich grate. Besides, when you're cooking items, such as steaks or burgers, you will probably want the fire closer to the food, so you will raise the charcoal pan and set it on the charcoal pan brackets (custom upgrade on some of the units). With the pan raised, you can no longer flip the standard sandwich grate.

  This is where the flat grate comes in. On the BBQ26S and BBQ42 you can get by without a flat grate when you hook the top part of the sandwich grate onto the open lid. But even then, the flat grate is a little handier and you're able to close the lid when you're cooking to control your fire in case of flare-ups and capture some smoke.

Standard Grate Hooked Onto Lid

Flat Grate Over Raised Charcoal Pan

- **Griddle.** Turn your barbecue into an all-day event! Add this heavy steel griddle to any chicken cooker and you're ready to fry eggs, pancakes, sausage, bacon, and hash browns. Or have fun with burgers, fries, and anything else you can imagine frying!

- **Thermometer**. You can add a calibratable thermometer to a chicken cooker lid to monitor the temperature in the grill. Consider this option if you prefer cooking by a thermometer instead of by the amount of fuel. This upgrade is only useful if your chicken cooker has a lid.

BBQ42 Options

- **Insulated**. Insulation in the BBQ42 adds a sealed double wall to the firebox. (The lid won't be insulated.) With insulation, you should be able to cook three rounds of chicken with one load of charcoal, instead of one round. This means serious charcoal savings if you use it to cook multiple batches in one setting.

Meadow Creek uses a quality high heat paint, but these pits endure a lot of intense heat. Insulation eliminates the problem of paint peeling from heat on the outside of the firebox, so it will take less repainting and maintenance.

- **Charcoal Pullout.** The pullout is a drawer in the bottom of the pit. You can pull it out to add more charcoal or clean out the ashes. If you'll be grilling all day long, this option will be very useful. With a charcoal pullout and a flat grate, the BBQ42 could even smoke pork butts!

- **Solid Tires.** Swap out the pneumatic tires on your BBQ42 for a set of solid tires to eliminate the possibility of a flat.

BBQ26S Options

- **Hitch-N-Grill Bracket.** This bracket is a cool gadget for mounting a BBQ26S to the hitch of your truck or SUV. Please note that it doesn't work well on a mini-van loaded for vacation or any vehicle with a low hitch.

Trailers Only

- **Slideout Grates.** The slideout grates upgrade puts the grate on a track that slides over the side of the trailer for convenient loading and unloading. Standard grates normally have to be loaded elsewhere and carried to and from their cooking position by two people walking on either side of the trailer. This is hard to do if your trailer has a roof (because of the supporting frame), or when you're parked really close to a building or cooking alone. (Old style expanded metal grate shown.)

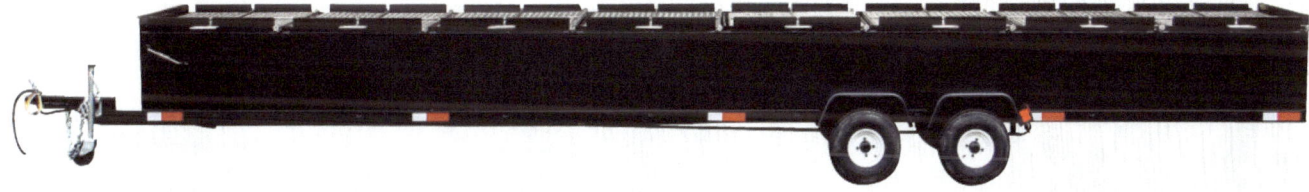

- **Additional Pits.** Need more cooking space? We can add as many pits to your trailer as you want.

- **Lids.** Without lids, it takes a lot of flipping when your fire gets frisky. The lids make fire control a breeze and virtually eliminate the stress when you're aiming for perfect results. In some places, you may also be required to cook with the meat covered. Lids solve that problem too. The lids upgrade on the trailer pits includes a double partition between the pits to make room for the lids.

Miscellaneous Options

- **Stainless Steel Lid.** The stainless steel lid turns the chicken cooker into a nice work table (when it's not hot, of course) if you have it on a trailer with other equipment. This upgrade also adds the perfect accent to a stand-alone insulated BBQ42.

- **Taller Lid.** Think you might want more clearance above your flat grate sometimes? Consider a taller lid. A taller lid increases clearance by 4" in the BBQ26S and 5" in the BBQ42.

Pig Roaster Options

Meadow Creek pig roasters are super versatile with a straightforward "personality." They offer fewer upgrade options than the Meadow Creek smokers, yet they can smoke or grill anything you can throw on them.

The charcoal pullout (for charcoal-fired models) is the most popular of all the pig roaster options. Next are doors in lid, second tier grate, vinyl cover, and grill pan. We'll cover these first.

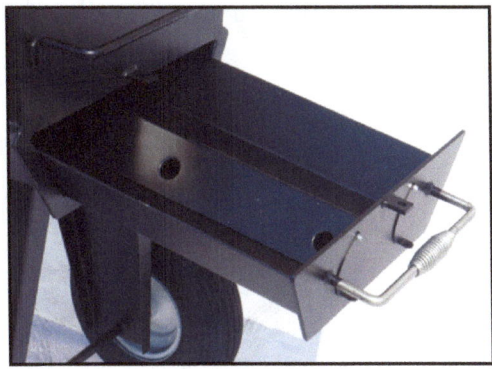

Charcoal Pullout

Doors in Lid

- **Charcoal Pullout.** The pullout is a drawer in the bottom of the cooker that slides out of the end. It's perfect for adding more charcoal during the cook without opening the lid and removing the grate and drip pan. Plus it helps protect the bottom of your pig roaster from excessive heat. (For charcoal-fired models only.)

- **Doors in Lid.** These little doors on the front side of the lid let you see and reach inside the cooker without opening the lid and losing so much heat. (Not available on the PR36.)

- **Second Tier Grate.** The second tier grate sits on top of the main grate and nearly doubles your cooking surface for smaller items such as ribs, briskets, and pork butts. It's a great investment if you're going to cook a lot of foods beside whole pigs.

Second Tier Grate

- **Charcoal Grill Pan.** Sometimes you might want to cook with direct heat. This grill pan turns the pig roaster into a hungry charcoal grill for cranking through hundreds of burgers, hot dogs, steaks, or whatever your heart desires.

Grill Pan

Chip Tray

Charcoal Pan Insert for Gas Models

- **Charcoal Pan Insert.** There is a charcoal pan for both charcoal and gas models.

  If you pass on the charcoal pullout, consider the insert to make clean up easier. This pan sits in the bottom of the roaster and holds the ashes. To access the pan, you will remove the cooking grate and the drip pan. When you're done cooking, simply lift it out the top. It also adds another layer of steel under the fire, increasing the life of your pig roaster.

  The charcoal pan for gas models straddles the burner and lets you fire the cooker with charcoal. There is a series of holes along the top for cooking with charcoal and gas at the same time. For example, you could start the cook with charcoal/wood to give your meat some smoke flavor; then, once it starts dropping in temperature, turn on the gas for the rest of the cooking period.

- **Rib Rack.** Want to cook a pile of ribs? This rack holds ribs on edge so you can cook more at one time.

- **Solid Tires.** Upgrade the pneumatic tires on your pig roaster (non-trailer models only) to a set of solid tires to eliminate the possibility of a flat.

Rib Rack

- **Chip Tray.** The tray is 1' x 2' and sits on top of the burner (gas models only). It lets you add wood chips to generate light smoke in the roaster. Also consider the charcoal pan insert with holes above the burner (explained above) for more smoke in your gas pig roaster.

- **Propane Gas Tank.** We offer a 43-pound tank without OPD and 30 or 40 pound tanks with OPD. They ship empty. You'll need a tank if you choose a gas model, but you may choose to get one locally.

Tank Smoker Options

Meadow Creek's tank smokers come with standard features that you'd have to pay extra for on many other brands, such as sliding stainless steel grates. You can deck them out even further with a long list of upgrades, including insulated firebox, stainless steel work shelves, and a sweet trim package.

- **Mounted Chicken Cooker.** You can add a chicken cooker (BBQ26S or BBQ42) to the front of any TS trailer. This is a popular upgrade because it lets you grill things like chicken or sausage while you cook low and slow.

- **Trim Package.** The trim package adds a touch of class with aluminum wheels and fenders and a stainless steel smokestack. Sharp!

Mounted Chicken Cooker on TS120

Trim Package

- **Stainless Steel Shelves.** This upgrade replaces the standard expanded metal shelves with solid stainless steel. They keep juices from dripping down into hard to reach areas and are easy to clean. Besides, they look amazing!

- **Jerky Racks.** This rack slides into the glide where the regular grate goes and is made of evenly-spaced rods to hold jerky strips.

Stainless Steel Shelf

Jerky Rack

- **Extra Grate in Smoker.** Adds a third glide (permanent) and grate in the cooking chamber. Would be great for cooking thin items that don't need much vertical space. You can easily remove the middle grate for projects where you need more space.

Extra Grate in Smoker

- **Extra Shelves in Warmer.** The warming box comes standard with three stainless steel racks. These extra racks give you more shelf space.

Live Smoke in Warming Box
Left: Stack on box
Right: Vent to control airflow from the firebox

- **Live Smoke in Warmer.** The warming box and firebox are separated with a solid piece of metal. Live smoke puts an adjustable vent from the firebox to the warming box and a stack on top of the warming box, so you can cook meat with smoke in the warming box. Without it, you can still cook beans on the very bottom or keep your cooked meat warm.

- **Insulated Firebox.** If you'll be using your smoker a lot, you can pay off the insulation in a short time by charcoal savings alone. The amount of charcoal you save varies, but normally it will take 40–50% less charcoal.

The smoker temperature will be more consistent in cold weather, which means more fun cooking and cranking out awesome barbecue year-round!

Even though Meadow Creek uses high-heat paint, the paint has a hard time holding up where the heat is intense. With an insulated firebox, the firebox paint will last much longer because the outside will not get as hot. You will have less maintenance to do.

Insulated Firebox

Insulated Firebox Door

- **Charcoal Grill Pan.** The grill pan slides into the glide for the bottom cooking grate and holds charcoal for cooking things like juicy burgers with direct heat. A great choice if you want a smoker that can grill too.

- **Charcoal Slideout Basket.** This steel basket slides in a track in the firebox. It holds the coals away from the firebox walls, which helps extend the life of your firebox and the paint outside the firebox.

- **Rib Rack.** This rack holds ribs on edge so you can cook more at a time.

- **Stainless Steel Lid for Woodbox.** Makes a great table top. Available with or without hinges.

Charcoal Grill Pan

Charcoal Slideout Basket

Rib Rack on Standard Grate

Exceptions and Additions

- Trim package is not available on the TS70P and TS120P; however, you can add a stainless steel smokestack on these models.

- Warming Box is an upgrade on the TS70P and TS120P; included on the other tank smokers.

- Vinyl cover on the TS500 is custom; price is not listed on our website.

- Tandem axle with brakes is available on the TS250 and TS500. We add a tandem axle to your trailer if your configuration gets too heavy for one. The upgrade price includes brakes for both axles.

Tandem Axle

- You can swap the pneumatic tires on the TS70P with a set of solid tires to eliminate the possibility of a flat.

Custom Options

There are even more ways you can customize your smoker with "custom" options, upgrades with prices available upon request. These include an aluminum toolbox, mounted spare tire, or stainless steel warming box. Beyond that, you can quote a trailer with a custom floor plan with a fold-down roof and any configuration of grills and smokers you want.

SQ36 Smoker Options

- **Charcoal Grill Pan.** The grill pan works like the grill pan for the tank smokers, but hangs under the main grate instead of sliding in the glide of the bottom grate.

Second Tier Grate

- **Second Tier Grate.** The second tier grate sits on top of the main grate and almost doubles your cooking surface. A highly recommended upgrade.

- **Insulated Firebox.** See "Insulated Firebox" in the tank smoker section.

- **Solid Tires.** Upgrade the pneumatic tires to a set of solid tires to eliminate the possibility of a flat.

- **Rib Rack.** See "Rib Rack" in the tank smokers section.

- **Charcoal Slideout Basket.** See "Charcoal Slideout Basket" in the tank smokers section.

Box Smoker Options

- **Extra Grates.** The BX50 comes standard with 4 grates 6" apart. You can add 3 extra grates, which will reduce the space between the grates to 3". The BX25 comes with 3 grates approximately 4.5" apart. You can add 2 extra grates, which reduces the space to approximately 2.25". Full briskets and pork butts will not fit with all the grates in use, but it gives you more cooking area for things like ribs.

- **Stainless Steel Interior.** This replaces the painted interior with stainless steel for easier maintenance.

- **Rib Rack.** See "Rib Rack" in the tank smokers section.

- **Custom Color.** Standard color is black. You can upgrade to John Deere green, fire engine red, or blue.

Trailer Options

- **Fire Extinguisher Mount.** A mount with a strap for securing a fire extinguisher to a chicken cooker trailer.

- **Replacement Wheel and Mount.** It's always a good idea to have a spare wheel on hand. You can even add a mount to your chicken cooker trailer.

It's really important to compare apples to apples and not apples to lemons. It's often the details that determine whether an offset smoker is fun, cool, and easy to use. Here are seven marks of a smoker that will give you many years of dependable service and keep a smile on your face.

Stainless Steel Grates

Meadow Creek uses strictly food grade stainless steel for their food grates. This adds to the cost of your equipment initially, but you can rest assured that the investment will pay off in the long run. Stainless steel grates do not rust, so they make cleanup easier and eliminate any contamination from rusty grates. Unlike regular steel grates, which will likely be rusty before you cook on them once, you can clean these grates with a pressure washer or oven cleaner, and get them perfectly clean for the next run without worrying about rust.

Double Sliding Grates

Meadow Creek's tank smokers have at least two removable sliding grates. Some even slide out on either side for easier access—really sweet compared to setting the top grate on top of the bottom one.

Door Latches

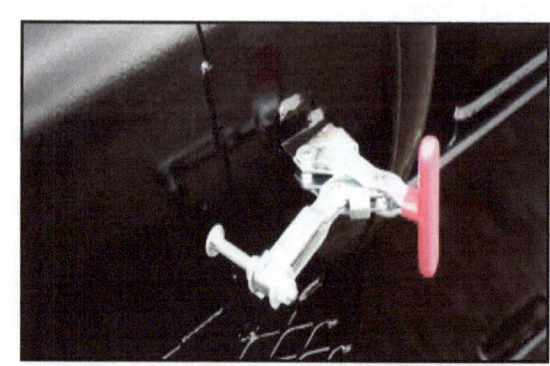

How many times have you seen smokers arriving at competitions and barbecue events with bungee straps on the doors? Meadow Creek uses positive lock latches that close the doors tightly and keep them closed.

Warming Box

Meadow Creek's smoker trailers come standard with a warming box. These are really handy to keep things warm while you finish smoking the ribs or cook beans on the top of the firebox. Upgrade it to live smoke to expand your cooking space. (See "Making Sense of the Options".)

Removable Ash Pan

Meadow Creek's smokers have a removable ash pan (drawer), which makes it easy to remove the ashes during or after your cook. There is a vent on each side of the firebox below the fire grate. Your fire will burn more consistently when the ashes in the firebox can fall through a grate into an ash pan and the air can draft up from beneath the fire grate.

Trailer License

Meadow Creek is a certified trailer manufacturer, though not all BBQ trailer makers are. Each trailer comes with a VIN number attached and a certificate of origin is available upon request, which makes it easy to register the trailer. You can rest assured it's road-safe with a professional design, road-worthy wheels, and LED lights.

Reverse Flow Draft

Meadow Creek tank smokers (TS models) have reverse flow draft and a curved tank end, which help a lot in maintaining consistent temperature throughout the cook and from one end of the smoker to another. (See "Meadow Creek Cooker Types" for more information on this feature.)

Backyard Smoker Comparison

Meadow Creek makes several fine backyard smokers. This chart illustrates the differences between the PR36, SQ36, and TS70P.

PR36

SQ36

TS70P

	PR36	SQ36	TS70P
Style	Vertical	Offset	Reverse Flow Offset
Summary	Versatile charcoal grill; smoking possible with standard grill pan	Great smoker; limited grilling possible with optional grill pan	High end smoker; grilling possible with optional grill pan
Features			
Stainless Steel Grates	✓	✓	✓
Thermometer	✓	✓	✓
13" Pneumatic Tires	✓	✓	✓
Firebox	X	✓	✓
Ash Pan in Firebox	X	✓	✓
Grate in Firebox	X	✓	✓
Smokestack	X	✓	✓
Drain Valve	X	✓	✓
Reverse Flow Draft	X	X	✓
Sliding Grates	X	X	✓
Front Work Shelf	optional	optional	✓
Water Pan	✓	X	✓

	PR36	SQ36	TS70P
Options			
Vinyl Cover	✓	✓	✓
No Flat Solid Tires (set)	✓	✓	✓
Rib Rack	✓	✓	✓
Additional Grate	✓	✓	✓
Charcoal Pullout	✓	X	X
Charcoal Pan Insert	✓	X	X
Charcoal Grill Pan	standard	✓	✓
Insulated Firebox	X	✓	✓
Charcoal Basket	X	✓	✓
Stainless Steel Shelf	✓	✓	✓
Warming Box	X	X	✓
Extra Shelf in Warmer	X	X	✓
Live Smoke in Warmer	X	X	✓
Jerky Rack	X	X	✓
Stainless Steel Stack	X	X	✓
Size Differences			
Cooking Area	3.4 sq. ft. with optional grate: 6.47 sq. ft.		6.85 sq. ft. with optional grate: 10.28 sq. ft.
Crowd Size (based on pork butts)	50–75 people	50–75 people	100—175 people

This article explains the differences between the PR36, SQ36, and TS70P illustrated in the chart above.

PR36 vs. SQ36

The key difference between the PR36 and SQ36 is the cooking style. The SQ36 has an offset firebox, while the PR36 has a vertical arrangement, with the fire in the bottom of the cooking chamber. The drip/grill pan included with the PR36 hangs between the fire and the cooking grate to create indirect heat. Either model can cook with direct heat grilling or indirect low and slow.

When it comes to direct heat grilling, the PR36 is more versatile than the SQ36 because you can grill from the grill pan, about 6 inches from the food. Or you can remove the grill pan and build a fire in the bottom of the cooker with the fire about 12 inches from the meat. The greater distance is important for some items, such as bone-in chicken.

In the SQ36, you can only grill in the optional grill pan because of the smoke diffuser in the bottom. While you can still grill about anything you want by banking the coals to one side, the PR36 is the better option for you if you're planning to grill most of the time.

If you're mostly looking to do low and slow, the SQ36 would be a better option because it has a more indirect heat source, which makes it easier to master amazing ribs and other tricky foods.

Because the PR36 doesn't have a firebox, you can add an insert which sits in the bottom of the grill, or a pullout, which slides into the end of the grill for adding more fuel without removing the grate. You can upgrade the SQ36 to an insulated firebox with a sliding charcoal basket.

SQ36 vs. TS70P

If you've been researching the SQ36 and TS70P smokers, you might have wondered why the TS70P is more than twice as expensive as the SQ36. Here are the reasons:

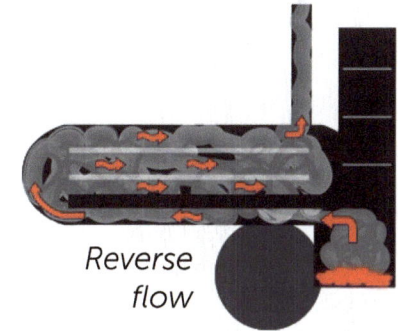

Reverse flow

1. The TS70P smoker uses reverse flow draft to help keep the heat and smoke evenly distributed throughout the cooking chamber. Before entering the cooking area, the smoke and heat travel through a channel below the cooking chamber to the opposite end of the tank. The smoke reverses its direction as it enters the cooking chamber and moves through the cooking area and finally, exits the smoke stack on the same end as the firebox. The SQ36 has a distribution channel for the smoke in the bottom and center of the cooking chamber, where the smoke goes from the firebox into the cooking chamber and then out the stack on the end opposite the firebox.

2. The TS70P can be upgraded to add a warming box above the firebox for keeping food warm. The live smoke option lets you cook meat in the warming box by adding a vented opening from the firebox.

3. The TS70P smoker has a built-in pan under the bottom grate for water smoking. The pan can hold one gallon of liquid. You can use water or apple juice in this pan to increase the humidity in the cooking chamber. The SQ36 does not have this pan so the drippings go to the bottom of the smoker.

4. The TS70P smoker is easier to clean up than the SQ36. The TS70P's drip pan catches the drippings and slants to the center with a V groove running down the center. This groove funnels liquid to a drip stem with a ball valve outside the smoker. The SQ36's smoking chamber is not as easy to clean out since the bottom is flat with the distribution channel in the middle.

5. The TS70P has sliding grates. The 2nd Tier Grate adds more cooking space to the SQ36, but the 2nd Tier Grate sets on top of the bottom grate, making it a bit less convenient to flip the meat on the bottom grate.

6. The TS70P comes standard with a work shelf along the front side. The SQ36 doesn't have a shelf, but you can special order it with one.

7. A standard TS70P smoker with two grates has 6.85 square feet of cooking area. The optional third grate gives you a total of 10.28 square feet of surface. The SQ36 with the optional 2nd Tier Grate has 6.47 square feet of cooking area.

8. The TS70P smoker has a heavier cooking chamber than the SQ36 smoker. The TS70P cooking chamber is 3/16" thick and the SQ36 uses 13 gauge (3/32" thick) metal. Both are impressively solid.

9. Without add-ons, the TS70P weighs 535 pounds, while the SQ36 weighs in at 310 pounds. As you can see, the TS70P comes with a couple hundred more pounds of steel than the SQ36. One advantage of the SQ36 is that it's more mobile, especially on uneven surfaces.

BX50 Cabinet Smoker

This chart illustrates some of the differences between two cabinet smokers—the Backwoods Competitor and Meadow Creek's BX50. The following article explains the differences in more detail.

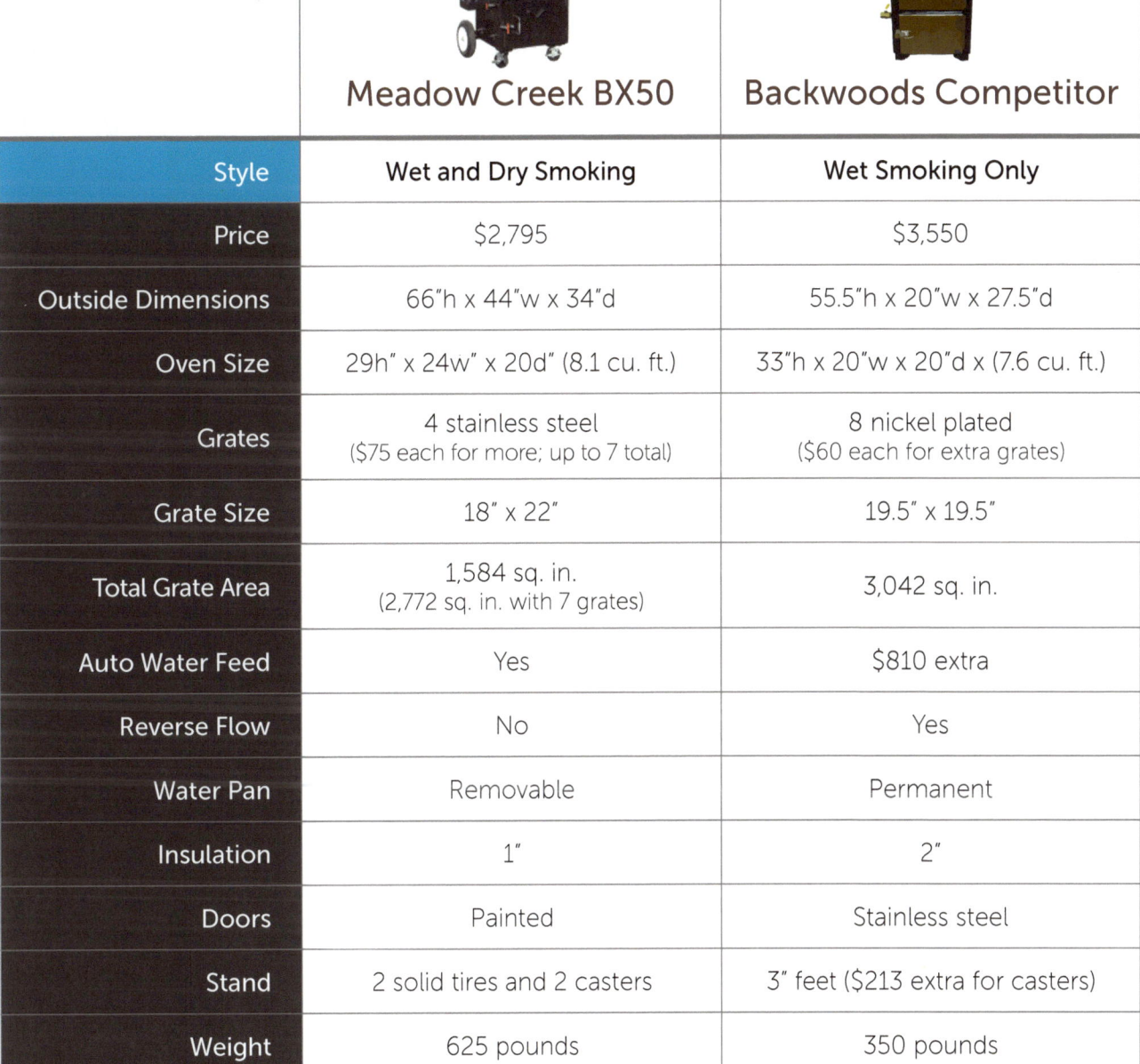

	Meadow Creek BX50	Backwoods Competitor
Style	Wet and Dry Smoking	Wet Smoking Only
Price	$2,795	$3,550
Outside Dimensions	66"h x 44"w x 34"d	55.5"h x 20"w x 27.5"d
Oven Size	29h" x 24w" x 20d" (8.1 cu. ft.)	33"h x 20"w x 20"d x (7.6 cu. ft.)
Grates	4 stainless steel ($75 each for more; up to 7 total)	8 nickel plated ($60 each for extra grates)
Grate Size	18" x 22"	19.5" x 19.5"
Total Grate Area	1,584 sq. in. (2,772 sq. in. with 7 grates)	3,042 sq. in.
Auto Water Feed	Yes	$810 extra
Reverse Flow	No	Yes
Water Pan	Removable	Permanent
Insulation	1"	2"
Doors	Painted	Stainless steel
Stand	2 solid tires and 2 casters	3" feet ($213 extra for casters)
Weight	625 pounds	350 pounds

🛈 Check current prices online. The prices above are listed to compare the two models and may have changed.

By comparing the BX50 with the Backwoods Competitor, we don't mean to bash the Backwoods smokers; they make fine smokers. Our intention is to show you how much value the BX50 offers for the money.

Wet and Dry Smoking

The Backwoods Competitor requires water or liquid in the pan to stabilize the smoker temperature. The BX50 is built for wet or dry smoking, which means you can use it for jerky and other foods that need a dry smoke environment.

Size and Weight

On the outside, the BX50 is much bigger and weighs 275 pounds more than the Competitor. The BX50 is a beast and you will probably want help rolling it up and down a trailer ramp. The weight proves you're getting a lot of steel for your money.

Capacity

The BX50 oven is 0.5 cubic foot larger and each grate is 15.75 square inches bigger, which is really not much difference in the whole scope of things. However, the Competitor does have more cooking area out of the box since it ships with 8 grates.

The Competitor ships with 8 removable grates 3" apart with the option to add more grates. The BX50 Box Smoker comes with 4 removable grates 6" apart. You can add 3 extra grates for a total of 7, which reduces the grate spacing to 3". The Competitor's 8 grates offers almost 300 square inches of cooking area *more than* the BX50's 7 grates. This extra cooking surface would be useful for thin items such as ribs; however, for thicker items, such as full briskets and pork butts, you will need more than 3" spacing.

Comparing our meat capacities with the Competitor, it looks like there is not much difference. For example, they list 8–12 briskets. We list 2 briskets per grate, times 4 grates, which equals 8. We list 16 pork butts; they have 16–18. We list 4 racks of baby back ribs per grate, which equals 28 racks when using 7 grates. They list 22–26 slabs of baby back ribs. Since the BX50 grates are bigger, the only way they are getting more capacity is by using more grates or crowding the grates more.

Auto Water Feed

The BX50 comes with a 5-gallon water jug that keeps water in the pan. This is really helpful if you don't want to hassle with opening the smoker door and checking the water level on those long cooks.

Air Flow

The Competitor is reverse flow, and some people have wondered how the BX50 air flow is designed. The BX50 is not reverse flow; however, it is insulated and produces very consistent temperatures in the oven. In our experience, the top and bottom thermometers show only several degrees difference once it's up and running, at least when using it as a water smoker.

The BX50 is an upright smoker with the fire box in the bottom and a water pan, steel plates, and a grease pan separating the fire from the food.

Here is a break-down of the air flow:

- The air enters the firebox through vents on the sides of the firebox. The vents make it easy to fine-tune your fire and hold a consistent temperature for a long 8–12 hour burn.

- The water pan sits directly above the fire. It slides into the smoker on the left side of the firebox. Two latches hold it in place on the outside.

- Above the water pan is a solid plate of steel with 1" holes around its perimeter.

- Above the first plate of steel is another plate of steel, with a round pattern of holes in the center.

- The grease pan slides in above the second plate of steel, diffusing the heat even more. The air flows past the grease pan in the front and back.

- Now we are in the cooking chamber where the food is. The smoke stack is at the top of the cooking chamber, in the middle of the ceiling. The air enters the stack left and right, traveling through a short horizontal channel, then up and out.

Water Pan

The Competitor's water pan is permanently welded into the smoker to keep it from warping. It must have water in it for the smoker to maintain a stable temperature. The BX50 water pan is removable and held securely by positive lock latches on the outside of the smoker. It is heavy enough that it will not warp or burn through if you run it dry.

If you have any questions about the Meadow Creek BX50 Box Smoker or any of their equipment, fire away! We'll be happy to help.

Meadow Creek Versus Lang

Perhaps you're stuck between Meadow Creek and Lang. Here are some of the differences between a Meadow Creek tank smoker and a Lang.

Ash Pan

Meadow Creek Offset Smokers have a sliding ash pan in the firebox. The pan makes it easy to remove the ashes while you are cooking or after the burn. In a Lang, the ashes fall onto the bottom of the firebox.

Rounded Ends

Both Lang and Meadow Creek tank smokers have a reverse flow configuration. Lang uses steel pipe with flat ends welded onto the ends. Meadow Creek insists on using tanks with rounded ends for better air circulation.

Latches

Lang uses a lever-latch on their smoker doors. Meadow Creek smokers have adjustable, positive-lock latches on all the doors. They are cool and fun to use, and you can be sure your doors will never pop open while bouncing down the road—even without using bungee straps.

Grates

Lang's grates are regular steel that will likely be a little rusty the first time you open the door, and most of them are not sliding, although these features are available for extra cost. All Meadow Creek cooking grates are food-grade stainless steel with a 25-year warranty against rusting. Grates that don't rust make clean-up and maintenance a lot easier and eliminate all posibility of rust contamination on your food—besides it's just really cool to have shiny grates! Both the top and bottom cooking grates on a Meadow Creek tank smoker are sliding, which is a huge plus for adding and removing food.

VIN Number

Meadow Creek is a certified trailer manufacturer and each trailer comes with a VIN number for registering it as a trailer.

Options

Lang offers a fair amount of options, but Meadow Creek specializes in offering upgrades, such as insulated firebox, stainless steel work shelves, and live smoke in the warming box. (See "Making Sense of the Options".)

Warming Box

Meadow Creek's smoker trailer models come with a warming box that you can use to cook beans and keep meat warm or upgrade with live smoke for more smoking room. Lang has warming boxes on some of their models.

Excellence

Langs are rugged and built to last, but from what we have seen and heard, they are overall more crude and the builders are not as picky with their cuts. The team of craftsmen at Meadow Creek gives a lot of attention to detail in the cuts and welds. They grind sharp corners and welds smooth and go the extra mile to achieve superb quality.

When comparing prices, remember to take everything into consideration, as comparing base prices straight across will not give a fair picture. Stainless steel grates, warming boxes, and outstanding craftsmanship are not free.

- Do you want the "Cadillac" of the smoker industry?
- Do you want grates that won't rust?
- Do you want an elite cooking experience, attention to detail, and knock-your-socks-off craftsmanship?

Choose a Meadow Creek smoker and proudly support the revolution Meadow Creek has brought to the barbecue world.

Combination Trailers

How about multiplying the potential of your new barbecue trailer by adding a second or third cooker? A sink and extra storage space might come in handy too!

Ultimate Caterer Trailers

Almost any scenario can be part of your trailer design, including chicken cookers, pig roasters, smokers, grills, sinks, gas stoves, deep fryers, and storage.

- Heavy duty road-worthy frame and suspension with 2-5/16" ball hitch
- Electric Brakes
- Optional hinged roof system with the following:
    - Vented ridge
    - Aluminum diamond plate 4' wings
    - Gas spring assist lift
    - Superior bracing locks down roof in transit or up while in use

Your Meadow Creek dealer can provide a custom floor plan and help you design the barbecue trailer of your dreams.

Caterer's Delight Trailers

The Caterer's Delight gives you a pig roaster and a BBQ42 chicken cooker on a trailer. There are four different possibilities on the pig roaster: PR60, PR60G (gas), PR72, or PR72G (gas).

Tank Smoker
With Mounted Chicken Cooker

Meadow Creek can add a BBQ42 or BBQ26 chicken cooker to the front of your TS120, TS250, and TS500 smoker trailer.

See "Types of Meadow Creek Cookers" and "Cooking Styles" for more information on these smokers and grills.

How to Order

We sell our products exclusively through our dealer network. Use the dealer search on our website to find a sales rep to work with. Our dealers are trained to answer your questions, provide quotes, and help you choose the smoker or grill that's best for your needs.

All of our dealers stock some inventory, but we also drop-ship a lot of orders. If your dealer doesn't have the unit you want in stock, ask them about having it shipped to your location or a nearby freight terminal.

If you have trouble finding a dealer or getting the help you need, please email us at info@meadowcreekbbq.com. You can also get a wealth of information about our products on our website at MeadowCreekBBQ.com.

Meadow Creek Welding, LLC
New Holland, PA
Email: info@meadowcreekbbq.com
Website: MeadowCreekBBQ.com

Warranty

Meadow Creek offers a warranty against defects under normal service for one year from the date of the original sale. The stainless steel grates have a 25-year warranty against rust and weld failure. Read the full warranty on our website at www.meadowcreekbbq.com/warranty.

Specs

Are you wondering how far the grate is from the charcoal pan or how many BTUs a gas pig roaster is rated? You can download a detailed spec sheet for each of the models when you go to that product's page in our online product catalog.